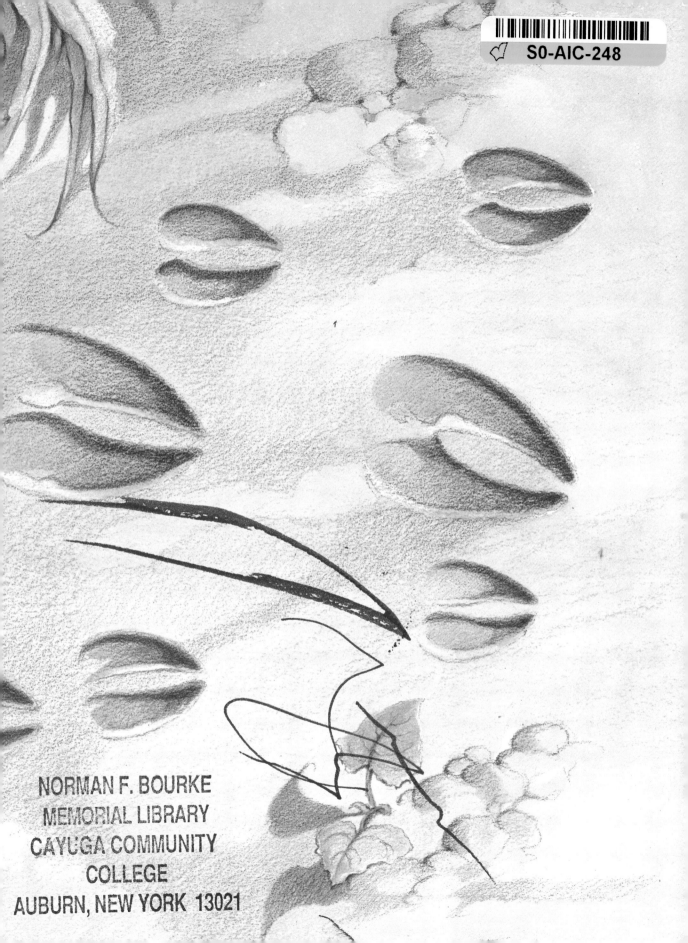

To Harold Kraushar,
a man whose eyes brighten
whenever he sees a deer

Library of Congress Cataloging in Publication Data   Arnosky, Jim.   Deer at the brook.   Summary: A poetic and pictorial portrayal of the lovely things that happen at a brook as a mother deer and two fawns come to drink, fish leap, and sunlight sparkles on the water.   1. Deer—Juvenile literature. [1. Deer. 2. Animals]   I. Title.   QL737.U55A76   1985   599.73'57   84-12239   ISBN 0-688-04099-3   ISBN 0-688-04100-0 (lib. bdg.)

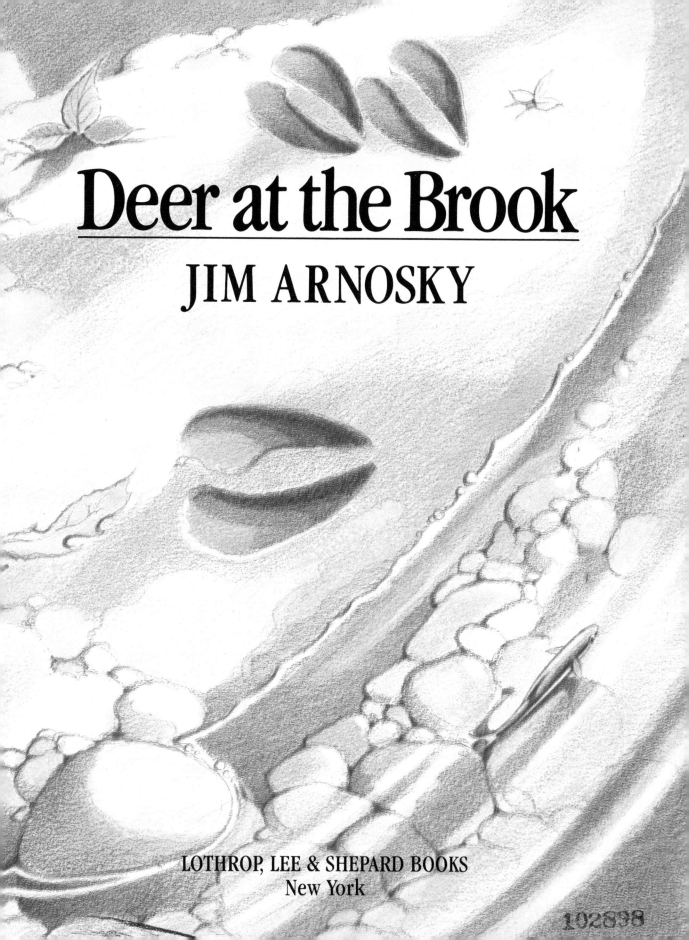

Deer at the Brook

JIM ARNOSKY

LOTHROP, LEE & SHEPARD BOOKS
New York

The brook is a sparkling place —
sunlight on water, water on stones.

The brook is a place
deer come to.

Some come alone.

Some come together.

Mothers bring their fawns
to drink...

and to eat.

They walk in the water.

They watch the fish leap.

They play on the sandy bank

and nap in the sun.

Sunlight on water, water on stones—

the brook is a sparkling place.

DATE DUE

JUN 3 0 2008		
SEP 23 2011		
OCT 19 2011		
GAYLORD		PRINTED IN U.S.A.

Juvenile